'AVANTI!' GRADED READER SERIES

Dario, dove abit

Elio Guarnuccio and Michael Sedunary

Illustrated by Neil Curtis

CIS Educational

CONTENTS

You're wasting your time and money. It's cheaper to buy a copy of this book than to photocopy it!

INTRODUCTION

The aim of the **Avanti! Graded Reader Series** is to provide our students with reading material at a level of language well within their grasp. These really do purport to be readers that young students can handle alone, comfortable in their familiarity with the central characters and the vocabulary they use.

A feeling of familiarity, yes, but there will also be the pleasure of breaking new ground. We see the **Avanti!** characters in new situations, relating to some new characters: Dario at home with his menagerie of pets; Laura away for the weekend on her uncle's farm, Giorgio doing battle down at the local **sala giochi.** Similarly, the language used will take the students slightly beyond what has been mastered in the text, giving them the opportunity to extend their vocabulary and their understanding of the language.

Individual reading for pleasure is an important and rewarding activity but these readers are also ideally suited for use as classroom texts. They lend themselves to all the uses to which a teacher may put the cartoon scripts of **Avanti!**: reading aloud, acting out, making audio or video tapes etc. Similarly the written exercises could be set as tasks to be performed by the whole class.

From the practical point of view these readers provide several benefits to the teacher. They supply ideal supplementary material for those students whose background or ability place them in need of extension work. They offer the opportunity for quiet reading periods in a week which might otherwise be packed with hectic oral interaction. There are up to fifty written exercises in each reader giving students plenty of scope for quiet reinforcement of language points they are studying.

The teacher may therefore give particular attention to some students while others are working from the readers. To help in this situation we have provided correction cards so that students can check their answers with minimal assistance from the teacher. These correction cards are available separately.

Most importantly these readers are intended to provide a good, entertaining 'read' in Italian. As with the **Avanti!** text the aim has been to make the characters **simpatici** and the situations humorous in an effort to motivate students to go on improving their Italian.

**Buona lettura e buon divertimento!
Michael Sedunary and Elio Guarnuccio.**

UN CONO E UNA CASSATA

Buongiorno a tutti. Io sono il signor Bono.
La signora Casati non c'è oggi.
Non sta molto bene, sta molto male.

Sta male? La signora Casati sta male? Mi dispiace!

Hi, hi, hi. La signora Casati non è a scuola. Che miracolo!

Silenzio. Come ti chiami?

Mi dispiace signor Bono. Mi chiamo Giorgio.

Mmm, Giorgio.

Attenzione a Giorgio. È alto e forte ma è bugiardo e molto cattivo.

Mmm, Giorgio.

Io mi chiamo Angela.

Io sono Faye . . .

ESERCIZI

A. Vero o Falso? After reading the first chapter you have to decide whether the following statements are true (vero) or false (falso).

1. La signora Casati non c'è oggi.
2. La signora Casati sta molto bene oggi.
3. Dario è in ritardo oggi.
4. Il cane ha l'influenza.
5. Il pesce non è contento.
6. Il signor Bono non è a scuola.

B. Sta bene o sta male?
After reading this chapter you should know whether these characters are feeling well or not. Make up your mind and write **sta bene** or **sta male** for each one.

Modello: Sta male. 1.    2.

3.    4.    5.

C. Who fits the description?
Write down in Italian which character was described in the following words:

Modello:
strong   Giorgio è forte.

1. late   4. intelligent   7. sad
2. shy   5. tall   8. small
3. tired   6. bad   9. liar

D. Opposites!
Write down a word or expression that has the opposite meaning to the following:

1. contento   4. bravo   7. intelligente
2. in tempo   5. bene   8. buongiorno
3. piccolo   6. in ritardo   9. ragazzo

E. Choose one of the adjectives from this chapter to describe the following pictures:

Modello: stanca

F. A scuola o a casa? At school or at home?
Write a short sentence explaining whether the following are at school or at home.
Modello:
Il banco. *Il banco è a scuola.*

1. La signora Casati.   4. Il pappagallo.
2. Il signor Cono.   5. Il cane.
3. Faye.   6. Kevin.

UNA CASA O UNO ZOO?

A. Quanti animali! What a lot of animals!
What do Italians call these animals? Use the word <u>un</u> (a, an) in front of each one.
Modello: <u>*un pappagallo.*</u>

B. Che pappagallo! What a parrot!
How did Dario's parrot say the following things:
1. Hi beautiful!
2. What's your name?
3. Angela is beautiful.
4. Silence, stupid!
5. Aren't you sick?
6. Where's the school bag?

C. Buongiorno, ciao, buonasera, buonanotte, arrivederci, a domani.
Use each of the above greetings only once. Which would you use when . . .
1. You go to a friend's place after school and your friend's mother opens the door.
2. As you arrive at school you meet one of your teachers.
3. Some relatives are leaving after visiting your place for the weekend.
4. You've been talking to a friend after school, but now it's time to get onto your bus.
5. You meet a school friend down the street on Saturday morning.
6. It's late at night and your parents tell you to go to bed.

D. Basta per oggi! Che miracolo! Mi dispiace! Avanti! Mamma Mia!
<u>Ecco! Attenzione! Silenzio, stupido!</u>
Use each of the above exclamations only once. Which would you use when . . .
1. You're playing tennis and you hit your opponent with the ball.
2. You serve an ace with your second serve.
3. The person on the next court is shy about coming over to pick up her tennis ball.
4. She can't see the ball caught up in the hose.
5. A dog is barking every time you go to play a shot.
6. Just when you thought you had the point won your opponent hits a great winner.
7. You're hot and thirsty but your opponent wants to play another set.
8. Your opponent is turning on the hose to water the court but doesn't realise
it's pointing at the club president.

E. How did they say . . .
Find out how the characters in chapters 1 and 2 expressed the following:
1. I am Mr. Bono. Mrs. Casati isn't here today.
2. I am Faye. I'm small and shy.
3. You are Laura and you are Dario.
4. I am not Dario. He is small and very shy.
5. His name is Tagliatelle. He's lovely, likeable and very big.
6. Here's the house now. Come in!

F. Talking about girls . . .
Notice that when Dario was saying that Faye is small he said, "Faye è piccola."
The masculine -o ending has changed to the feminine -a ending.
How would you say . . .
1. Faye is shy.
2. Angela is likeable.
3. Laura is beautiful.
4. Mrs. Casati is tired.
5. Angela is naughty.
6. Faye is not tall.

G. There are three adjectives in these chapters which end in -e.
These adjectives don't change. They end in -e whether you're
describing a boy or a girl. Write down these three words. They mean:
1. intelligent.
2. strong.
3. sad.

H. How did they say . . .
1. Do you have a dog?
2. I have a parrot, a fish . . .
3. Do you have a house or do you have a zoo?
4. I have a dog.
5. I have a dog too.
6. Dario, are you home?

I. Come si chiama . . . ?
These questions relate to characters
in the 1st and 2nd chapters.
1. Come si chiama il cane di Dario?
2. Come si chiama il cane di Faye?
3. Come si chiama il ragazzo alto, forte e cattivo?
4. Come si chiama il ragazzo intelligente?
5. Come si chiama la maestra?
6. Come si chiama il maestro?
7. Come si chiama il papà di Dario?

LA CAPRA E IL COMPITO D'ITALIANO

Mamma mia, ho un compito d'italiano per domani. Il signor Bono non è simpatico. Dov'è la mia cartella?

Tagliatelle, dov'è la cartella squa, squa Tagliatelle . . .

Ah, sì, Tagliatelle ha la mia cartella. Dammi la cartella, per favore, Tagliatelle. Per favore, dammi la cartella.

Non ho la cartella.

Pinoooo! Hai la mia cartella? Dov'è la mia cartella?

Ma Dario, non lo so. Io non ho la cartella, ma ecco il quaderno.

Che disastro! Mamma, mamma dov'è la mia cartella?

Non lo so Dario, ma ecco il libro d'italiano. Ed ecco la penna e la gomma.

Ah no, la capra. Dov'è la capra?

Nanna, smettila! Basta! Dammi la mia cartella!

A. Vero o Falso?

After reading chapter 3 you have to decide whether the
following statements are true (vero) or false (falso).

1. Dario ha un compito d'italiano per domani.
2. Il signor Bono è simpatico.
3. Tagliatelle ha la cartella di Dario.
4. Pino ha la cartella di Dario.
5. Pino ha un quaderno.
6. La mamma di Dario ha il libro d'italiano.
7. La capra si chiama Nonna.
8. Dario è in ritardo a scuola.
9. Il quaderno di Dario non è molto bello.
10. La capra sta male oggi.

B. Use the correct word for 'the' (the definite article) with the following.
You have to choose either **il**, **la** or **l'**.

1. compito
2. cartella
3. quaderno
4. libro
5. gomma
6. astuccio
7. capra
8. cane
9. penna
10. pappagallo
11. elefante
12. ragazza

C. My, my!! The Italian word for 'my' is **mio** or **mia**.

Use **mio** with masculine words (the ones you use **il** with) and **mia**
with feminine words (the ones you use **la** with). Notice that Italians use the
word for 'the' then the word for 'my', e.g. **il mio libro; la mia penna**.
Write out the following expressions using **mio** or **mia** to fill the gaps.
Then write what the expression means.

Modello:

il <u>mio</u> quaderno   <u>my exercise book.</u>

1. la . . . scuola
2. il . . . pappagallo
3. il . . . pesce
4. la . . . capra
5. il . . . coniglio
6. il . . . astuccio
7. la . . . cartella
8. il . . . banco
9. la . . . sedia
10. il . . . quaderno

D. How did they say . . . ?

Write down the Italian expressions that Dario used to say the following:

1. I have an Italian assignment for tomorrow.
2. Ah yes, Tagliatelle has my school bag.
3. Pino, do you have my school bag.
4. I have a parrot and a fish.

Now use a fluorescent pen to highlight the Italian words
that mean 'I have', 'you have' and 'has'.

E. Write the Italian for:

1. my house
2. my homework
3. my pencil
4. my dog
5. my cat
6. my schoolbag
7. my desk
8. my chair
9. my school

F. Choose an expression from the right-hand column to answer those in the left-hand column. Rewrite them in your exercise book.

1. Dov'è il mio quaderno?
2. Dammi la cartella, per favore!
3. Il mio cane sta male oggi.
4. La capra ha il compito.
5. Ecco un gelato!
6. Sono in tempo oggi?
7. Il cane è molto brutto.
8. Sei stupido, sei brutto, sei . . .

1. Non è bello ma è simpatico.
2. Mi dispiace.
3. Grazie.
4. Ma non ho la cartella.
5. No, sei in ritardo.
6. Che disastro!
7. Ecco il quaderno!
8. Smettila! Basta!

G. Match the drawings with the word describing them, then write a complete sentence for each one. Remember to make the adjectives agree with the nouns.

Modello: 1. Giorgio è forte.

ATTENTI AL CANE!

ESERCIZI

A. Use the correct definite article il, la, l' with the following:

1. maiale
2. finestra
3. armadio
4. porta
5. video
6. televisione
7. sacco
8. uccello
9. influenza
10. mattina
11. sedia
12. banco

B. After reading the whole chapter, what do you think of Tagliatelle. Make your answers complete Italian sentences, beginning with sì or no.

1. Tagliatelle è un maiale?
2. Tagliatelle è timido?
3. Tagliatelle è forte?
4. Tagliatelle è un bravo cane da guardia?
5. È stanco?
6. È intelligente?

C. Che cos'è?
Write down the Italian word for the things pictured below.
Don't forget the definite article!

1.
2.
3.
4.
5.
6.
7.
8.
9.

D. Unjumble these sentences:
1. Guardia da Tagliatelle un è non cane.
2. Sacco favore per il apri!
3. Raro il forse è pappagallo molto.
4. Tu leva sempre la hai.
5. Quaderno favore dammi il per!
6. Una uno hai hai zoo Dario casa o?

E. Che disastro! Per favore! Cretino! Presto, andiamo! Niente!
Un momento! Apri la porta! Basta, smettila!
Which of these expressions would you use if . . .
1. Your friend is dawdling and you want to get moving.
2. Your brother won't give you any chips because you haven't been asking nicely.
3. You don't want to be hurried, you want to take your time.
4. Your brother is carrying on like a real idiot.
5. You're in a really sulky mood and someone asks what's wrong.
6. Your brother starts throwing sand at you.
7. Now he locks you out of the house.
8. You get back from the shop and realise that you've lost a five dollar note.

F. Dario's dad was being pretty mean to Tagliatelle early in this chapter.
See if you can translate into English what he was saying about Dario's dog.

DARIO CASANOVA

ESERCIZI

A. <u>Vanessa è troppo intelligente per la scuola.</u>
Vanessa is too intelligent for school.
If you put <u>troppo</u> in front of an adjective it means 'too . . .'
Make up an Italian sentence with <u>troppo</u> + adjective to describe the following people:
Don't forget: **-o for boys, -a for girls, -e for both.**

Modello:

Anna sits in a corner and never talks to anyone.

Anna è troppo timida.

1. Bruno can't come on excursion because he just fools around and causes trouble all the time.
2. We'll never beat them if Melissa plays. She doesn't even have to jump and she still reaches higher than any of us.
3. I'm never playing cards against Claudio again. He always gets the best cards. Always!
4. You can't expect Mum to take us bowling now. She has worked all day and now she needs a rest.
5. It's no use trying to get our dog Fido to do any tricks, he just hasn't got a clue what you're talking about.
6. I've tried everything I can to beat Gina. I have to admit I'm not up to her standard yet.
7. Every time Paolo gets lollies or chips or something, he ends up giving them all away to his friends.
8. Antonio tries hard but he really doesn't have a chance against those big kids.

B. <u>Sì o no?</u>
In complete Italian sentences write answers to the following questions.
Begin your answers with <u>sì</u> or <u>no</u>.

Modello:

Dario ha un pappagallo?

Sì, ha un pappagallo.

1. Giorgio ha una ragazza?
2. La ragazza di Giorgio è a scuola?
3. Vanessa lavora a K Mart?
4. Angela è alta e bionda?
5. Angela è bella?
6. Dario è sempre in tempo?
7. Il pappagallo ha l'influenza?
8. Angela è la ragazza di Dario?

C. **Write the following words with the correct definite article:**

1. regalo
2. astuccio
3. televisione
4. elefante
5. scuola
6. uccello
7. cane
8. compito d'italiano
9. matita
10. gatto
11. influenza
12. astuccio

D **Write the Italian for:**

1. my cat
2. my homework
3. my bird
4. my school
5. my present
6. my desk
7. my television
8. my girlfriend
9. my boyfriend
10. my pencil
11. my teacher
12. my dog

E. **Giorgio and Vanessa get on very well at times, not so well at other times. Here is a list of things Vanessa said to Giorgio in the last week:**

Presto, andiamo!   Ti amo!   Basta, smettila!

Silenzio, stupido!   Mi dispiace!   Che disastro!

Now see if you can guess which expression she used in which situation. Each expression occurs only once.

1. Giorgio goes to pick her up at K Mart. Vanessa can't wait to get away from work.
2. Giorgio sees Vanessa at the other end of the supermarket and starts shouting out to her.
3. Giorgio runs over to talk to her and knocks down all the cans of dog food.
4. Vanessa spills half of her thick shake over Giorgio's new jeans.
5. Giorgio has a new water pistol and starts squirting her with it.
6. Giorgio tells Vanessa she is the most beautiful girl in the world.

F. **Your Italian grandfather is picking you up at school today. He's never been to your classroom before so you leave a note for him describing the room just in case you're still doing sport when he gets there.**

Here are some helpful expressions:

La mia aula è . . . → My classroom is . . .

La mia professoressa si chiama . . . → My teacher's name is . . .

c'è → there is

ci sono → there are

nell'aula → in the classroom

sul muro → on the wall

DRACULA E LA GALLINA BUGIARDA

Ciao, Dario. Come stai?

Angela! Ciao! Sto molto bene, grazie. Avanti, avanti!

Senti, Dario. Io non ho un video a casa ma ho un film molto interessante. Tu hai un video?

Sì, sì. Ho un video. Come si chiama il film?

"Dracula e la gallina bugiarda".

Mmm, interessante! Molto interessante!

Ciao, bello. Come ti chiami?

Mi chiamo Pino. Sono il piccolo fratello di Dario. E tu chi sei?

Sono Angela.

Ah, Angela. Tu sei la ragazza di Dario.

Che cosa?

Niente, Angela, niente. Andiamo.

Ecco il video, Angela. Dammi il film, per favore!

Ma Dario, che cos'è? Un pappagallo?

No, sono un coniglio. Angela è bella, squa. Ti amo, squa.

Silenzio, stupido! Mi dispiace, Angela. Il pappagallo è . . .

A. Sì o no?

In complete Italian sentences write answers to the following questions.
Begin your answers with <u>sì</u> or <u>no</u>.

1. Dario sta bene oggi?
2. Angela ha un video a casa?
3. Dario ha un video?
4. Pino è grande?
5. Dario ha un coniglio?
6. Il pappagallo è bugiardo?
7. La gallina è bugiarda?
8. Il film è interessante?

B. How did they say . . . ?

1. Angela: Hi, Dario. How are you?
2. Dario: I'm very well thanks. Come in. Come in
3. Angela: I don't have a video at home. Do you have a video?
4. Angela: Hi there, handsome. What's your name?
5. Pino: My name is Pino. I'm Dario's little brother.
6. Pino: You're Dario's girlfriend.
7. Dario: Give me the film, please.
8. Dario: Who is it? Is it Dracula's girlfriend?

C. Can you write subtitles?

Here is a short scene from the famous comedy-thriller <u>"Dracula e la gallina bugiarda"</u>.
When it is shown on TV it will need English subtitles. You've got the job.
Characters: Dracula, Ugo, La Gallina.

Ugo:	Buongiorno, Dracula. Come stai oggi?
Dracula:	Sto male, molto male. Ho l'influenza e non sono contento.
Ugo:	Mi dispiace.
Dracula:	Basta, cretino. Smettila! Dov'è la gallina?
Ugo:	Ecco la gallina.
Dracula:	Non è una gallina, stupido, è un pappagallo. Presto, andiamo. Apri la porta! Ciao, gallina. Andiamo a casa. La mia casa è molto bella.
La Gallina:	No, oggi sono troppo stanca.
Dracula:	Presto, Ugo, dammi il sacco.
La Gallina:	Arrivederci.

D. Bravo, brutto, intelligente, bugiardo, simpatico, bello, cattivo, forte, in ritardo, interessante, triste, grande, piccolo, timido, alto, biondo, contento, stupido.

These are the adjectives we have seen so far. See if you can write Italian sentences about people you know using as many of these describing words as possible.

Modello:  *Angela è brava.*

E. Match the following words

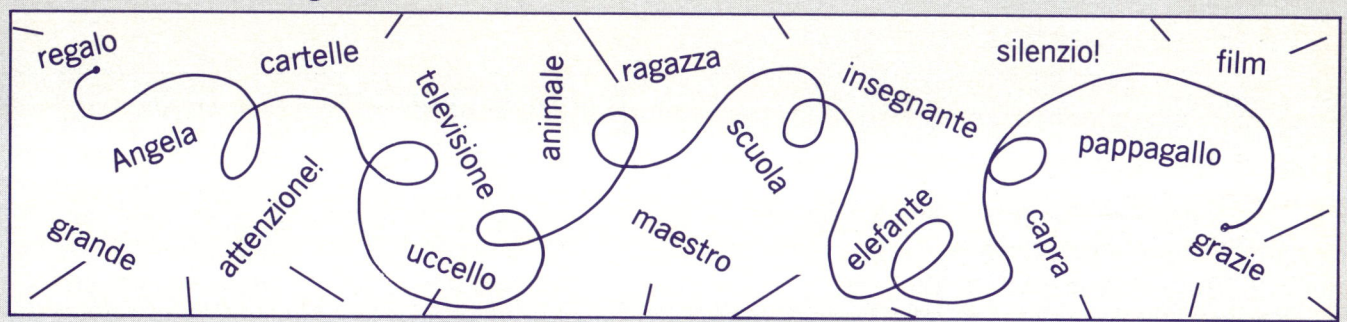

regalo cartelle ragazza silenzio! film
Angela televisione animale insegnante pappagallo
grande attenzione! uccello scuola maestro elefante capra grazie

F. In the spaces below, fill in the answers to the following questions. When you have done this, you will find in the vertical column Dario's favorite place in Florence. Discover what it is and find a picture of it.

All the words in the puzzle are in Italian.

1. You get it at school but you do it at home.
2. You'd say it if you were pleasantly surprised. Che ...!
3. If you're not quite ready you'd say Un ...!
4. Come in!
5. Also.
6. Another word for ciao.
7. Now.
8. He stars in the video Angela has.
9. Here is.
10. What!
11. Non è contento.
12. A kind person often has this characteristic.

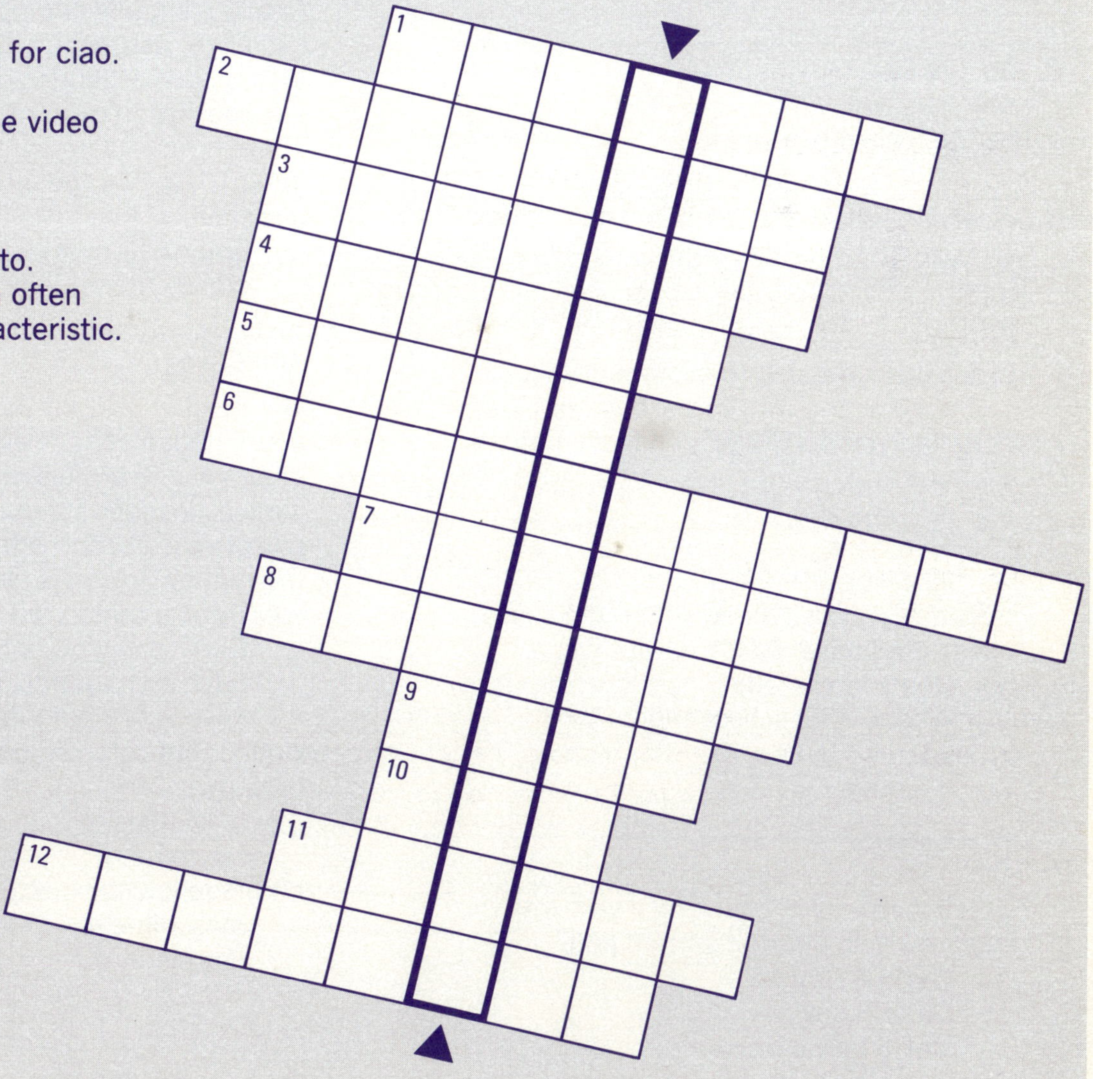

SUMMARY OF LANGUAGE POINTS

1.
sono	I am
sei	you are
è	he/she/it is

You use **sono** when you are talking about yourself (i.e. first person).
e.g. **Sono in ritardo.** I'm late.
You use **sei** when you are talking to someone (i.e. second person).
e.g. **Sei sempre in ritardo?**
    Are you always late?
You use **è** when you are talking about someone (i.e. third person).
e.g. **Dario è sempre in ritardo.**
    Dario is always late.
You also use **è** when talking about things.
    È una casa o uno zoo?
    Is it a house or a zoo?

2.
ho	I have
hai	you have
ha	he/she/it has

3.
io	I
tu	you
lui	he
lei	she

In English we always use pronouns like I, you, he or she with verbs. e.g. I am, he is. In Italian you don't always have to use the pronouns.
e.g. **è**   he/she/it is
    lui è he is
    lei è she is
Italians don't use the word for it in cases like those above. So it's always just **è**.
e.g. **Dov'è la cartella?**
    Where's the school bag?
    È lì.
    It's there.

4.   **Non** Not

The Italian way of changing a verb into the negative is to put **non** in front of it.
e.g. **Dario è timido.**
    Dario is shy.
    Dario non è timido.
    Dario isn't shy.

5.   **Asking Questions.**

Asking questions in Italian is very easy. You don't change the words at all. If you are writing you just put a question mark at the end of a sentence. If you are talking you put the question mark in your voice, i.e. you change your tone of voice to make what you are saying sound like a question.
e.g. **La casa è grande.**
    The house is big.
    La casa è grande?
    Is the house big?

6.   **The Italian noun.**

Italian nouns belong to one of two groups. They are either *masculine* or *feminine.*
Nearly all nouns ending in **-o** are masculine.
e.g. **libro, astuccio, gelato.**
Most nouns ending in **-a** are feminine.
e.g. **matita, penna, riga**
There is also a large group of nouns ending in **-e**. These may be either masculine or feminine.
e.g. **limone** (lemon) is masculine
    classe (class) is feminine

7.   **Adjectives.**

The most important thing to remember about Italian adjectives is that they match or agree with the people they describe. If a male is described then the masculine adjective is used. If a female is described the feminine form is used.
e.g. Dario è timid**o** ma intelligent**e**.
    Dario is shy but intelligent.
    Faye è timid**a** ma intelligent**e**.
    Faye is shy but intelligent.
Notice that some adjectives follow this pattern:
    masculine **-o**
    feminine **-a**
others follow this pattern:
    masculine **-e**
    feminine **-e**

SUMMARY OF LANGUAGE POINTS

8. | **The definite article – the.**

In English we have only one definite article – the word the. In Italian **il** is used with masculine singular words and **la** is used with the feminine singular ones.

e.g. **il libro**   the book
      il limone   the lemon
      la matita   the pencil
      la classe   the class

If the Italian word starts with a vowel, the **l'** is used whether the word is masculine singular or feminine singular.

e.g. **l'astuccio** the pencil case
      l'aula   the classroom

9. | **Molto.**

When **molto** is before an adjective it means **very**.

e.g. **Sono molto stanco.** I'm very tired.

When **molto** means **very** it never changes its ending, it always ends in **-o**.

e.g. **Giorgio è molto stanco.**
      Angela è molto stanca.

10. | **Come ti chiami?** What's your name?
Mi chiamo . . .   My name is . . .
Ti chiami . . .   Your name is . . .
Si chiama . . .   His/her name is . . .

11. | **Come stai?** How are you?
Sto bene.   I'm well.
Stai bene.   You're well.
Sta bene.   He/She is well.

12. | **The days of the week.**
lunedì, martedì, mercoledì, giovedì, venerdì, sabato, domenica.

Note: In Italian the days of the week are not written with a capital letter (unless they begin a sentence).

13. | **Di.**

In Italian there is no such thing as **'s** at the end of a word to say who owns something. You always have to use the word **di** which means **of**. So to say Dario's dog you say: **Il cane di Dario**. The dog of Dario.

14. | **il mio/la mia.**

When Italians use **mio/mia** to mean my in English, they nearly always put **il/la** before them.

e.g. **Il mio ragazzo.**
      My boyfriend.
      La mia cartella.
      My school bag.

Notice that like all adjectives it matches the noun.

VOCABOLARIO

A

a	to, at, in
adesso	now
alto	tall
amo	I love
ti amo	I love you
anche	also
anch'io	I also, me too
andiamo!	let's go!
animale (m)	animal
apri!	open!
armadio	cupboard
arrivederci	goodbye, see you later
astuccio	case, pencil case
attenti	beware
attenti al cane	beware of the dog
attenzione!	attention!, be careful
avanti!	come in, go on, come on!

B

basta!	that's enough!
bello	beautiful
bene	well
biondo	blond
bravo	good, bravo!,
bravo!	well done!
brutto	ugly
bugiardo	liar
buonanotte	goodnight
buonasera	good evening, good afternoon
buongiorno	good morning

C

cane (m)	dog
capra	goat
cartella	school bag
casa	house
a casa	at home
cassata	ice cream
cattivo	bad, naughty
c'è	there is
che ..!	what ..!
che cos'è?	What is it?
chiamo	
mi chiamo	my name is
ti chiami	your name is
si chiama	his/her/its name is
come	like, as
com'è?	how is it?
compito	homework
coniglio	rabbit
cono	cone
contento	happy
cosa	what
che cosa	what
cos'è?	what is it?
cretino	idiot

D

da	
cane da guardia – watchdog	
dammi!	give me!
di	of
il cane di Dario – Dario's dog	
il compito d'Italiano – the Italian homework	
disastro	
che disastro! – what a disaster!	
dispiace	
mi dispiace – I'm sorry	
domani	tomorrow
a domani	see you tomorrow
dopo	after
dormi tu?	are you sleeping?
dove	where
dov'è?	where is?
Dracula	Dracula
due	two

E

e	and
è	is
ecco	here is, there is
ed	and
elefante	elephant

F

favore	
per favore!	please!
film (m)	film
finestra	window
forse	perhaps, maybe
forte	strong
fortunato	lucky
fratello	brother

G

gallina	chicken
gatto	cat
gelato	ice cream
generoso	generous
giorno	day
gomma	eraser
grande	big
grazie	thank you
guardia	
cane da guardia – watchdog	

H

ha	he, she, it has
hai	you have
ho	I have

I

il	the
in	in
influenza	flu
insegnante	teacher
intelligente	intelligent
interessante	interesting
io	I
italiano	Italian
d'italiano	of italian

VOCABOLARIO

L

la	the
lavora	he, she works
leggi!	read!
leva	lever
lì	there
libro	book
lo	the
lui	he

M

ma	but
maiale	pig
male	not well
mamma	mum
mamma mia!	good grief!
matita	pencil
mattina	morning
mi dispiace	I'm sorry
mio	my
miracolo	miracle
che miracolo!	what a miracle!
molto	very
momento	moment
un momento	just a moment

N

niente	nothing
no	no
non	not
non lo so	I don't know

O

oggi	today

P

pappagallo	parrot
penna	pen
per	for
per favore	please
pesce (m)	fish
piccolo	little, small
porta	door
presto!	hurry!

Q

quaderno	exercise book
quanti	how much
Quanti animali!	What a lot of animals!
quasi	almost

R

ragazza	girl
la mia ragazza	my girlfriend
ragazzo	boy
raro	rare
regalo	gift
ridicolo	ridiculous
ritardo	in ritardo late
ritardo **in ritardo**	late

S

sacco	bag
scuola	school
scusi	I beg your pardon
sei	you are
sempre	always
senti!	listen!
si chiama	his, her name is
signora	Mrs, madam
signor(e)	Mr, sir
silenzio!	quiet!
simpatico	likeable, cute
smettila!	stop it!
so	I know
non lo so!	I don't know
sono	I am
sta	
sta bene	he, she is well
sta male	he, she is unwell
come stai?	how are you?
sto bene	I'm well
stanco	tired
stupido	stupid

T

tagliatelle	a type of pasta; the name of Dario's dog
televisione (f)	television
tempo	time
in tempo	on time
ti chiami	your name is
timido	shy
triste	sad
troppo	too, too much
tu	you

U

uccello	bird
uffa!	gosh!
un	a, an
una	a, an
uno	a, an

V

va	he, she goes
vento	wind
video	video

Z

zoo	zoo

REVISION CROSSWORD

All the words in the crossword are in Italian.

Across

5. pencil case.
7. Attenti _ _ cane.
8. First half of Dario's brother's name.
10. a little: un _ _
11. Nothing.
12. Signor Bono says this when the class isn't listening.
14. The initials of the character on the front cover of this book.
15. _ _ gatto.
16. _ _ maestra.
17. Non tu
18. _ _ amo!
21. A description of Giorgio.
22. _ _ cartella.
24. The opposite to **no!**
25. But
26. Angela è _ _ _ _.
27. Vanesse è la ragazza _ _ Giorgio.
28. It's watched by Dario and Angela.

Down

1. Dario's has a big mouth!
2. Buongiorno Signore. Come _ _ _?
3. _ _ sono felice.
4. Another name for Signor Bono.
6. Tagliatelle.
9. Non è stupido.
10. You write with them.
13. Come _ _ chiama?
17. Dario's problem.
18. Non io.
19. You say it if you disagree.
20. Angela, Laura e Faye sono _ _ _ _.
23. Two like nanna.
24. You sit on them.